# New Tantrism
## Introductory Themes

Klaire D. Roy

Translated from the original French version by
Josée Di Sario

Printed and bound in Canada by Imprimeries Transcontinental, August 2007

©*New Tantrism — Introductory Themes*. Klaire D. Roy

Volume ISBN: 978-1-896523-56-9
Collection ISBN: 978-1-896523-57-6

©Paume de Saint-Germain Publishing
Montréal, Québec, Canada, 2007

Registration of copyright: Third trimester 2007
National Library of Québec
National Library of Canada

Paume de Saint-Germain Publishing©
235 René Lévesque Boulevard East, Suite 310, Montréal, Québec, Canada H2X 1N8
Telephone: (514) 255-8700 ~ Facsimile: (514) 255-0478
E-mail: info@palmpublications.com;
Web site: http://www.palmpublications.com

Graphic Design: E.K., Eric Mathieu
Page layout and typesetting: Louise Roy

©All rights reserved. No part of this book may be reproduced in any form without permission in writing from the author, except to quote or photocopy specific passages for the purposes of group study.

**English books by Paume de Saint-Germain Publishing:**

- *Conclave of the Cryptic 7*. Klaire D. Roy. Volume I. 2007.
- *The Spiritual Science of Essential Yoga: Techniques of Meditation, Mantrams, and Invocations*, Volume I. Sri Adi Dadi. Compiled by Martine G. Fortier. 2004.
- *Brahman's Egg, Scriptings of the Soul in Question of Light*, Volume I. Sri Adi Dadi. 1995.

**French books by Paume de Saint-Germain Publishing:**

- *Le Rugissement du Lion de Montréal*. Klaire D. Roy. 2006.
- *Le Projet des 7*, Tome I. Ekeena Iothe. 2004.
- *Voyage au cœur de l'âme – La Voie de la Connaissance*, Tome 2. 2003.
- *La Voie… à pleine Voix – Inspiré de l'enseignement de Sri Adi Dadi*. 2002.
- *Dadi Jyoti, L'Éveil d'une Lumière Infinie*. Bhai Bibi Mataji. 2001.
- *Namaskar – Lettres à Dadi (24 avril 1994 - 26 janvier 1999)* Tome II. Bhai Bibi Mataji. 2001. Second Edition in Print.
- *La science des asanas-mudras – techniques dhyanam, dynamiques et invocatoires*, Tome I. Enseignées par Sri Adi Dadi. 2001.
- *La Voie de la Connaissance – Quelques percées de Lumière inspirées de l'enseignement de Sri Adi Dadi*, Tome 1. 1999.
- *Foudre Divine… Parfum de Rose*. Josée D. Senécal. Second Edition in Print. 1995.
- *Namaskar à mon Guru*, Tome I. Bhai Bibi Mataji. Second Edition in Print. 1995.

**Forthcoming books in English:**

- *Conclave of the Cryptic 7*. Volume II. Klaire D. Roy.
- *Namaskar – Letters to Dadi (April 24, 1994 - January 26, 1999)* Volume II. Bhai Bibi Mataji.
- *New Tantrism*, Volume II. Klaire D. Roy.
- *The Era of Ray 7*. Klaire D. Roy.
- *The Lion's Roar*. Klaire D. Roy.
- *The Spiritual Science of Essential Yoga: Techniques of Meditation, Mantrams, and Invocations*. Volume II. Sri Adi Dadi. Compiled by Martine G. Fortier.

**Forthcoming books in French:**

- *La science des asanas-mudras – techniques dhyanam, dynamiques et invocatoires*, Tome II. Enseignées par Sri Adi Dadi.
- *Le Projet des 7*. Tome II. Klaire D. Roy
- *L'Ère du Rayon 7*. Klaire D. Roy.
- *Nouveau Tantrisme*. Tome II. Klaire D. Roy.

**Forthcoming books in Russian:**

- *Conclave of the Cryptic 7*. Volumes 1 and 2. Klaire D. Roy.

# Table of Contents

Prologue

Introduction

The Impact of Ray 7 on Women .................1

The New Light of Mankind ....................3

Mankind Must Become that Which It "Is" ........7

Becoming the Perfect Note ....................11

Tantrism Incites Man Towards His Perfection .....15

The Role of the Tantric Master ................17

Pseudo-enlightenment and its Illusions .........21

The Impact of Tantrism on the Ego .............25
and the Personality

The Soul's Choices .........................27

Tantrism and Resistance .....................29

Tantrism Educates the Soul ...................33

Evolution Takes Place With the Group ..........35

Tantrism Is Not a Crutch for Our Evolution .....37

We Are Not "Innocent" ......................39

Being ....................................41

Autonomy versus Independence ...............43

The Ashram is not Autonomous ...............45

Verify Your Innermost Motivations ............47

Sexuality Within Tantrism ...................51

The Misuse of Sexuality .....................57

Growing Through Sexuality ..................61

| | |
|---|---|
| Understanding Sexuality | 63 |
| Man's Unconsciousness | 65 |
| Solitude Through Tantrism | 67 |
| Attachment and Autonomy | 71 |
| Tantrism Cannot be Understood Logically | 75 |
| Doubt | 77 |
| Acceptance | 79 |
| Inconstancy | 81 |
| Tantrism is Unique and not Buddhic | 83 |
| Consciousness | 85 |
| Don't Let Doubt Get You! | 89 |
| The Goal in Creating Man | 91 |
| The Extinction of Humanity | 95 |
| The Process of Rejuvenation | 99 |
| Eternal Youth | 101 |
| Duality | 103 |
| The Monad | 107 |
| The Ether | 109 |
| Perfection | 111 |
| The Kirpan Aspect | 113 |
| The Planes | 117 |
| The Illusion of Tantra | 119 |
| The Difficulty with Tantra | 121 |
| The Right Understanding of Tantrism | 123 |
| Epilogue | 127 |

# Prologue

Suffice it for you to know that I am Tibetan of origin and that my teachings aim to be more occult than mystical, since my work consists of awakening mankind so that he may become the bearer of his divine aspect. Mankind is not meant to live in ignorance. He is meant to become a conscious Light evolving within the cosmic plan of our planet. My task therefore, consists in transmitting to mankind the teachings that will allow him to become a free being, conscious of who he is and of what he is being called upon to become.

Djwhal Khul, The Tibetan

# Introduction

This book has been transmitted by the one we call the Tibetan. It is an introduction to the world of Tantrism. It in no way casts doubt on that which has already been written on the subject. However, it does allow us to cast a new look on a subject that is as old as the world. Since this book was dictated by D.K. in a sporadic fashion from August 2005 to June 2006, the treated subjects are not laid out in alphabetical order, but in the sequence in which they were received.

Klaire D. Roy

# The Impact of Ray 7 on Women

Today's woman is divided into two distinct energies, that of service and that which ties her closely to her ego. This phenomenon produces a discomfort within her that obliges her to become increasingly more demanding towards false needs that only satisfy the superficial aspects of her life. We are here referring to the woman who is more and more subject to the energy of Ray 7. This Ray allows the expression of the highest creativity in an individual, but also the most egocentric. It is the Ray of freedom within form, but can also be the Ray that imprisons within form.

Having always been subject to the energy of Ray 6 during its era of influence, women are now trying to free themselves from its influence, albeit in an awkward fashion. The difficulty stems from the fact that the 6th Ray has made her a slave of her own self and of the needs of men, whereas the 7th Ray has made her a slave of her desires, tied to those of men.

In the coming years, woman's role will be of great importance, since she will allow humanity, through the secret that she holds within her, to make great strides towards its destiny. Nothing is easy for her. The world of illusion has opened up with all its powers that will henceforth taint her vision. In the future, woman will know how to destroy these illusions by using a discernment that she will have gained from her experience and from the errors she will have committed regarding the illusory powers of a false well-being that she herself will have created.

At this moment, woman attracts to herself experiences that complicate her life and that of others by increasing her desire to control her vital space in view of becoming more autonomous. Woman is not meant to be autonomous in the sense that she hopes to become. This autonomy is more of the masculine kind, whereas feminine autonomy goes through a different route, another expression. Woman must understand herself and expand her horizons towards the hidden face of her emotions that do not now express her true needs. Having been subject for millennia to masculine domination in relation to her material needs, making her too often a slave rather than a woman, today's woman attempts to find her place in this world by using tools that are not necessarily her own. She must develop her own power of autonomy by cultivating within herself the sense of balance of things and of polarities.

# The New Light of Mankind

We will now discuss the new tantrism, since the time has come for you to establish contact with yourself and within yourself, so that we may proceed towards that which needs to be done.

The time has come for humanity to awaken from the deep sleep that is upon it, or should we say, that is imposed upon it. It must take a giant step forward in order to extricate itself from the emotional stagnation that prevents it from progressing higher towards its intellectual apogee which, once the illusions of the emotional plane will have been understood and conquered, will lead towards a greater support from the Masters who will be able to better serve humanity for whom the centre will have changed perspective, if not direction. All must change within man so that his destiny can be accomplished. Children will be more intelligent but not necessarily wiser. They will have to cultivate this wisdom within themselves through the medium of meditation and of the obligatory building of the luminous channel, the anthakarana. Without this bridge of light that will unite them to their Higher Self, they will not be able to accomplish the task that awaits them. In a few thousand years suffering will disappear from this planet, which will by then have become sacred. Mankind will evolve in close rapport with the divine energy of the higher planes. He will discover his immortality, which will diminish the cycle of birth and death. Man is immortal in his essence, but a veil of which the usefulness is still indisputable, prevents him from seeing this divine aspect within himself. The fear of death is an important leitmotif in man's progress. This fear produces in him the need to change in order to survive and suffer less. In the future, mankind will progress and change without this fear, which will no longer have its reason for being. Then man's desires shall be at the level of the changes he will expect of himself. He will "know" what he needs to do in order to become more and more Light, because he will have "seen" this Light manifest itself repeatedly during his evolution. The memory of his past lives will be as easy to recall as it is easy to flip through a photo album. He will see the unfolding of his "life" cut up into a multitude of "sequences" representing lives in which he will have "learned" or "failed" the lessons that he needed to learn and assimilate. The cult of the no-cult will disappear, making room for a divine aspect of the world overseeing the form and the matter contained within this form.

Mankind will be aware of the luminous space that circulates between each atom and cell of his body, which will no longer be subject to the laws of destruction and aging. Having become "light" he will experience increasing expansion, in accordance with the Light of his Monad who will by then be Master of his life. He will become that aspect of the Monad that makes him closely resemble God in its infinitely tiny aspect. When the time will come for mankind to become the amplified energy of his Self via his body, he will understand that he never existed other than by an intemporal link with his Monadic God that is the infinitely small of that which is infinitely large. God does not exist, only his reflection within the mind of man creates this illusion. This reflection is neither "Him" nor anyone else. He is a "creation" of man, created in order to give himself a goal, a line of conduct, allowing him to put the divine stamp on everything that lives, since the true God is man who has yet to learn that he is "everything", because he is the matrix. This matrix forms not a superman nor a superGod. It forms that which is unnameable and inconceivable.

# Mankind Must Become that Which It "Is"

For man to become conscious means that he must organize within himself the different creative sources that are from that which is higher than him. He must probe the depths of his being in order to become inexhaustible joy, of which he is the bearer. This joy comes from the consciousness that is awakening to God, from the Divinity of his "Self" that is installing itself within the evolving being. Once he has attained it, man must share his state of ecstasy with those who can understand, and assimilate his light directly with that which characterizes him, that is, his luminous Monadic source that shines within that which makes him Divine.

Man must not doubt that which he is and that which he will become. He will "know" how to conquer the sacred spaces that are characteristic of the course for the one who "journeys" towards his authentic and true nature that is found outside of the human laws linked to this planet. Man will cease to be human when he will become the divine aspect that is hidden in all that expresses the grandeur of "he whom" we can neither know nor see since it has no existence in this sphere where everything is linked to form within matter. Being without form and without matter, it cannot but be dimly and indirectly perceived by the one who attempts to sense it and to define its nature.

Similar to man in his complexity, tantrism allows us to define the undefinable since it is insubstantial, without beginning and without end, perpetually present and constantly ignored. Tantrism cannot help but express via its breath, the tune of the silent melody that makes up each and every parcel of that which vibrates within us. We are the symphony that is never completed, never heard and never understood in its totality. We are this, and that aspect that perceives a fragment of this fascinating music that in the core of its being is characterized by a vibratory note that is more intense, more elevated within this symphony that is increasingly perfect and more and more complete and complex in its simplicity. Man will become the musician of his vibrational transformation through the changes he will harness, as his own symphony becomes subject to the benefits of the tantric breath within his existence.

The mind complicates everything with its attempts at understanding, whereas the key to authentic change resides in being able to listen to that which is and to that which must be heard, and doesn't reside in the logic of that which is said and pronounced. One must allow emptiness to integrate itself within the vastness of our consciousness and which doesn't depend on the intellect that has become intelligent. Becoming intelligent doesn't presuppose a strong conscious vibration. Intelligence is but the first step towards a consciousness that shines like a central sun within a Universe where all functions via the transparency of the Rays emitted by this luminous form. Intelligence is but a very weak reflection of this luminous consciousness that already shines, but that is veiled by an "egotistical" unconscious derived from attachment to the lower self.

# Becoming the Perfect Note

Tantrism belongs to the pathless path. That is, it is a path that rests on nothing, except the emptiness that characterizes each individual in the deepest aspect of each of his incarnations. This emptiness belongs to legend, the cellular legend, of those who have attained authentic enlightenment leading them to the doorstep of Mastery, where those Beings who have accomplished this journey are waiting for them. At this precise moment in which man is crossing this threshold without a guardian — since he is now his own journey, his own path, his own threshold — he becomes identical to the kind of person we refer to as "someone who knows" beyond form and words. All his cells vibrate to a new rhythm in which silence has made room for the vibratory sound that produced the beginning of this world. It is a note that is both heard and infiltrates the deepest recesses of cellular memory, which resonates to this rhythm.

Multiple notes will be heard in the future and these notes will create a fundamental renewal that will allow all of humanity to free itself from the earthly attraction that determines each of our incarnations. We will no longer be "alone"; we will have become the "Unique One". The perfect note, which will resound as far as the confines of the Universe will allow the simultaneous liberation of all the occult schools (and "ashrams") that are still prisoners of the clandestine world that underlies form. The White Brotherhood will no longer have its reason for being and will free its members who will then be able to evolve in a higher dimension.

This era of great change isn't yet at hand, but the day will come in which humanity, having become conscious, will step through the door in one unified step into the perfect world contained in the formlessness of the higher dimensions that oversee our planet. Our physical form will no longer be necessary. All that will remain is an embryo of our astral body that will be controlled by a strong and resistant etheric body. The Mental plane will be at its apogee and a thinking humanity will no longer be subject to the limiting worlds of the lower bodies, especially those of the physical and of the astral.

Man will be free and will weave the fibre of the superman via his now perfect and clear consciousness.

Having become useless, suffering will diminish to the point that man will have forgotten its existence and the reason for its existence. We will no longer belong to the kind of era in which transformation by fire, which requires pain and tears, is necessary in order to understand and to change. Being a slave to pleasure and to comfort, man can only free himself from this slavery by going through painful realizations. Pleasure and comfort are nothing but illusions. A perfect existence implies a path that is always ascending, marked with discoveries and surrender, all of which illumines us way beyond the world of form. Fullness replaces comfort, while joy transcends happiness and pleasure.

# Tantrism Incites Man Towards His Perfection

Within tantrism, man studies the depth of the faith that is within him, the faith that he has towards himself in relation to the man-God that he understands through his logic. Tantrism shrouds the thought of man in a thick veil that obliges him to face his True Nature that is far from being as perfect as he believes it is. Man is imperfect, and while knowing this, he ignores it or tries to ignore it. He only has himself to blame for the problems and confusions that lie on his path on his way to that which he defines as "my perfection", whereas he is already perfectly imperfect in his ultimate perfection. Tantrism kindles the fire of wisdom so that it surfaces and amplifies within this receptacle that inhabits the human spirit, which is on its way to being dehumanized. The perfection of man-God can only happen through the imperfection of this earthly world that dulls the consciousness of the being who inhabits it, because of its intense attraction. We are being called upon to free ourselves from ourselves and from everything that this implies.

# The Role of the Tantric Master

In our discussion of tantrism, we are considering an occult aspect of man's journey towards his perfection. We use the term "occult" since all that is hidden in man's behaviour, or to be more precise, all that man hides by his behaviour, must surface from its hiding place and reveal itself in the light of day. At the beginning this will be guided by a competent "Instructor" or a "Master" with whom the soul will join once an authentic contact has been made between man and his Atmic aspect.

Having been tainted by its proximity to man, the soul, being far from perfect, will not be able to accomplish the work of "un-occulting" man's behaviour by itself. It will need the Monad who will join Itself to the soul in order to allow a deeper work, a more genuine work. A good Master, an authentic Master has conquered his soul and now straddles the Monadic eagle. His flight is precise and direct and his vision, perfect, which isn't the case when contact has been established with the soul alone.

The tantric Master first works with the personality of man whose ego is king and master. When the personality softens and we can glimpse the glimmers of light that are the result of an ego that has been worked on and purified, the Master then grinds the personality in his hands in order to produce a glow that is even more real, more powerful, more genuine; this is the glow of the soul when man is undergoing transformation. The shaken ego finds itself diminished, without strength, at the edge of the abyss of his ignorance and supplicates the awakened Being that is asleep in him, to save him and to heal him.

When the sound of the ego's suffering finds the right note, the soul leans towards it and undertakes the work of cleansing. This can take several incarnations, in which suffering and deep despair will affect the life of man undergoing intense transformation. The ego shall not be saved but cleansed temporarily in order to allow man to continue with his journey on the "delicate" path that he refers to as his purification. He only purifies his ego and his personality. He doesn't actually purify himself. His Light improves but doesn't increase in strength. It will truly increase when the Monad takes over. Up until this point, man needs help from a "Master" who is more "awakened" than he is since the soul, far from being perfect, can cause man to err towards other paths where he will find a certain comfort due to his "purification", and which he will mistaken for enlightenment.

How sad that so many follow this path. We then find ourselves with man who has a head, a certain intelligence, but no wisdom and no heart. The "ego"-ism of man remains very much present, the soul not having been able to completely channel the energy of the wild horse that desires his space and freedom. The ego only cedes its place after the Monad has leashed it and guided it to safe ground where it will serve as a tool and not as a tyrant as it has been up until now.

# Pseudo-Enlightenment and Its Illusions

Tantrism isn't a path for the weak, as you know. One must be aware of this fact, because if you underestimate this path, you will go only as far as the edge of the forest, in other words, you will remain at the superficial level. To become a "profound" Being, one must dig deep within oneself and become a well of wisdom wherein is found all that we need to know about ourselves and purify that which needs to be eliminated from our consciousness in order that it can become clear, but above all, precise and active.

A clear but inactive consciousness only brings sadness and disappointment to the Masters who observe this "inaction" as being a weakness in humanity in regards to the comfort of the mind and the self-sufficiency of the egoic[1] being, which

---
[1] Refers to the ego.

is just beginning to discover its own light but that is at this stage, only a pale reflection of the true power of the authentic Light of a totally awakened being.

Being partially enlightened brings us nowhere. It is only a phase we must go through without abiding there. Enlightenment is Enlightenment, and anything that resembles it must be seen as such, a pale resemblance that gives us the taste for "the" Truth but that is in fact just an imperfect simile-image, incomplete, a deception.

One who is pseudo-awake can become a menace to those who truly are awakened. They become tyrants to those who are asleep, and a nightmare for those who are awakened. The "asleep" ones do not know that they are sleeping. They take their state of sleep for their reality and live this reality as if nothing else mattered. They are in error, and attempting to show them this "mistake" demands patience, courage and discernment. We don't wake someone in a brutal and unconscious manner, unless it is absolutely necessary.

These "semi-awakened" ones are on the path of discipleship, a path dimly lit, ill-defined and misunderstood. The too-powerful ego dominates the path and imbues each part of this path with its false image of reality. These beings become subtle tyrants to their entourage who receive their criticisms and judgments based on a false vision of someone who "knows" only part of the truth, without knowing its true nature.

Each phase has its illusions and the one who is just beginning to wake up is full of himself, filled with false concepts that he cultivates. Discernment is faulty, consciousness having been covered by thick veils acquired in incarnations in which he believed he was learning "more" while in fact "knowing less". This is not a paradox, but a fact: acquiring "knowledge" isn't about "knowing" or about "recognizing" the reality of that which encloses the mystery of that which is alive. True "knowledge" is the deepening of that which we are as perfectly imperfect beings journeying towards the perfection of this imperfection that translates into the true nature of man who is subject to terrestrial laws.

Enlightenment goes through Tantrism that shapes it, shakes it up and renders it Authentic. There exist many awakened pseudo-gurus who populate this Earth and who too often constitute a scourge for "those who know" and who are journeying in this way, that is, finding the authentic path and journeying it with wisdom and discernment.

# The Impact of Tantrism on the Ego and the Personality

The inner upheaval related to tantrism allows the human work to take place. All human aspects, good or bad, rise up to the surface in order to be studied, purified and eliminated. Nothing remains hidden and this terrifying aspect for human nature brings with it serious questioning.

This necessary self examination functions so that the ego and the personality remain present but in a way that their reason for being is continuously questioned. The use of their existence, the goal of their presence are put into question in order to perfect their true nature that is more a matter of the human existence of the soul than the soul itself.

# The Soul's Choices

The human soul is neither good nor bad. It is neutral as a whole, but taints itself according to the circumstances related to earthly life and to the desire of man to choose his path, which will be the middle path for the fearful and the lazy, and the right-handed path for the adventurous and passionate and those who seek the good in their nature and that of others. It is not a path for the weak of heart.

The left-handed path is unfortunately much used in the incarnation experiences, since it is the easiest path and that which seems to bring the greatest satisfaction of the self, but not of the Self. This path through which journey millions of souls ready to experiment this ambiguous way with its different aspects, is a path where hatred, jealousy, rejection of others and finally of self, that is of one's divine nature, intermingle. This is a path to be avoided and one that causes the most damage to the soul, marring it forever with scars that will become a vibrational memory of those lives in which the soul played difficult and dangerous games for its own survival.

Tantrism, as a whole, allows the soul to reclaim its destiny through a shake-up of the ego performed by the hand of a "Master" in order to "awaken" the consciousness that is asleep on roads that are little recommended, roads that are paved by the personality and the ego, but roads that are used by the soul who desires to journey on the path that it deems the most propitious to experimentation.

The soul loves to experiment and this sometimes leads it on pathways that are not so "certain" and that delay its progress, since the soul evolves and it is a myth to believe that it is perfect and infinite. It possesses limits that it needs to respect if it desires to complete the work of perfecting that for which it came on earth to do.

# Tantrism and Resistance

The difficulty inherent in tantrism is our own resistance. The greater our resistance, the more it becomes difficult to apply the authentic aspects of tantrism in our lives. Tantrism is beyond any dogma, principles and all applications referred to as "conceptual". Tantrism is only concerned with the Atmic aspect of the individual via his personality.

Resistance is natural for human nature that has become crystallized in a material world that was conceived, from the beginning, in order to allow the soul to deepen its original "pure", but superficial essence. The soul in its infinitely small aspect, sees only the surface of things and does not at all apply itself to becoming more intense and more profound. It needs to learn, to experiment in order to integrate that which will become the true fiber of its existence, and this implies knowledge that comes from "God".

In relation to tantrism, the soul seeks to integrate it in its most subtle aspects while forgetting that tantrism cannot be integrated without fully being in a space-time where the soul no longer has a hold on the personality through which it experiments the energetic aspect of tantrism that manifests through man's "awakened" consciousness.

There comes a time in which there is a point of friction and the soul no longer has contact with the personality and goes through dark periods, since its temporary source of existential experimentation is no longer available.

When the personality is "polished" and purified to its maximum, it becomes the instrument "par excellence" that obliges the soul to purify itself and to advance towards the path of its own Light. No longer being a crutch for the soul, the personality becomes a point of support allowing integration of the true and deep nature of man, thereby allowing the soul to become fully human, fully profound and diversified within that which it integrates. "The human soul" returns to its source with lessons learned and which it can transmit to other souls who have not had the courage to experiment on Earth, the different aspects and qualities that the human aspect can bring to the Divine aspect.

When man is "realized" in his true nature, while remaining imperfect, he becomes an inexhaustible source of joy for the soul, but above all for the Monad who sees the positive effect that the human aspect has on the experience of the soul. Man is not superior to the soul; it is its physical counterpart that will one day allow the soul to realize itself more completely and perfectly.

The soul has much to learn, whereas man has everything to learn. We are the core of the soul, which in turn is the core of the Monad. Tantrism allows us to live this as a fact, while remaining in the physical existential world.

# Tantrism Educates the Soul

I do not advise you to logically define that which characterizes tantrism. This energy leaves in its wake a mystery that cannot be understood and unveiled until the soul has given itself over to that which is higher than itself. It must abandon its control in order to allow the energy coming from the Monad to imbue man's personality, now ready to adequately channel the design willed by the entity that we qualify as God.

Tantrism serves to educate the soul that is still much too young and too curious. It can destroy the ego, incontestable vehicle of the soul, but it cannot under any circumstances damage the soul, that is a Law. It must, however, awaken it and render it more compatible with its becoming, which no longer concerns the lessons learned on Earth.

Tantrism shakes up the ego and perturbs man's personality, but it must above all produce that spark of light that will allow man, via his soul, to accomplish its most ardent desire: to become complete and "one" with the "all". The soul is frightened, as is the ego, to vanish within this apprenticeship. It must be educated and elevated to the rank that is its heritage.

# Evolution Takes Place With the Group

I am disappointed by the attitude of certain students who believe that they know a lot, but who in fact know very little, and therefore they know nothing at all.

The most difficult path, that which is related to tantrism, is a path of authentic value and true honor. One must first of all be true to oneself in order to be so with others. The façade that we project is nothing but a deception that hampers the progress of the disciple and of the group.

You are not alone in your evolution, and the group is as important as the Master. The Master directs, corrects and activates the group, whereas the group supports, comforts and aids in maintaining the direction imposed by the Master.

The Master does not have a choice, he must "impose" a discipline on the disciple, otherwise nothing will be transformed. The Master's will and his perseverance are the mainstay for the disciple who is advancing by the projected Light of the Master's will who desires enlightenment for his disciple.

The group has enormous potential, but it is still too centered on itself, on its personal needs. Its vision is too short and too conditional. Each one advances on the path forgetting that he is not alone and that others accompany him. Group initiations are not "illusion", they exist and many are now ready to accede to this higher level; it is only their individuality that prevents it. They want the exclusivity on their initiation, whereas in the era of Ray 7, this will not be possible. The group has the place of honor and we must not forget that.

# Tantrism Is Not a Crutch for Our Evolution

I am not strict, I am exact in my words. Disciples of worth deserve that we give them attention and that we correct certain harmful attitudes.

The study of tantrism is an effective means by which to learn and not an excuse to be forgiven for an incorrect attitude. Tantrism is a driving force, a catalyst and not a crutch used to excuse ourselves for that which we really are. Tantrism destroys in order to transform.

It is not a "miracle" that cleanses everything as if by magic. It involves a whole lot of effort that leads to success for the one who knows how to work in the direction of the work demanded of him. If there is resistance, refusal to make the appropriate effort, the energy can turn back against the student and lead him to his ruin. He will experience hell on earth due to the illusions about himself that he will not have been able to master, but that on the contrary he will have cultivated.

Tantrism activates everything and distributes its energy efficiently in all the spheres of the student's and disciple's life who either "shines" by the Light diffused by this energy or collapses due to a misuse of the energy received.

Blessed is the one who studies tantrism under the loving and affectionate eye of a Master who knows how to intervene and correct an incorrect attitude. The entire responsibility of "correction" falls upon the Master, but the entire responsibility of the energy received and not digested by the disciple is his full responsibility.

The disciple is responsible for everything he experiences, and for how the energy from his actions affects others. He must at all times be conscious of this fact, and cease watching himself act in a self-centered manner. He knows that evolution is not easy, but who really complains except for the one who wishes just a superficial transformation without any suffering.

# We Are Not "Innocent"

It is futile to debate on important points when the consciousness is not open to receiving such information. One must therefore work without fail to open a consciousness that has become hardened and crystallized due to the fear of knowing too much, since this implies huge responsibilities towards one's self, but above all towards others.

We know much. We cultivate our minds, that is our lesser mind, since Mind isn't meant to be cultivated, but we forget the essential, that is that transformation implies forgetting one's self, but above all the releasing of expectations that falsify true seeing of that which needs to be "known" and that which needs to be "understood". Knowing a lot obliges us to have an authentic view turned towards self and towards the study of all that this implies. The responsibility of "knowing" makes it such that we are not "innocent" and much less "unconscious" of our actions.

# Being

Tantrism teaches the individual to know himself despite the false concepts he has cultivated in regards to himself. A direct seeing on his own reality reasserts the soul's will to better itself and to direct its essence towards that which is higher than itself.

"Being" implies going beyond what we believe to be the universal soul, as an incarnated soul in a world in which we have everything to learn, everything to understand.

Coincidence does not exist and "being" is therefore not the fruit of coincidence. "Being" what we really are requires a forgetting of that which we believe we are and a total absence of what we would like to "be". Tantrism is not to be defined, it simply is. We cannot learn how to "be" via tantrism, since tantrism is not "being" because "being" implies a notion of existence that tantrism is not.

Tantrism cannot be defined and it cannot define us. Attempting to identify tantrism would be like attempting to identify oneself to a false existence, since nothing is more false than trying to grasp onto the hope of being "tantric" in our "being", in our approach, because nothing could be more inaccurate than to try and define tantrism and much less to try and identify oneself in relation to tantrism.

I don't wish to discourage the seeker, I want to awaken him to the fact that nothing is more difficult than to journey on this path, since nothing is more false and more authentic. Tantrism seems paradoxical because we are paradoxical.

# Autonomy versus Independence

In these difficult times in which humanity is experiencing upheaval on so many levels, it would be well not to confuse autonomy with independence. The first is related to the soul via the personality and the second is simply related to the ego via the personality.

Being autonomous implies an openness towards others while avoiding being a useless burden. There is a harmony that installs itself that shows total respect towards others and others towards one's self. There is no distance, no constraints, no ego overflowing with pride nor a mind bent on protecting itself from the influence of others. There is a movement in two directions, from the interior to the exterior and from the exterior towards the interior. There exists a plenitude and a space where everything becomes possible.

A Master is autonomous and not independent. He transmits warmth and love, not coldness and separation. Which are you? Autonomous or independent?

One must first of all be independent before becoming autonomous, but the price to pay is steep; dependence and independence are similar, both imply a close link with the lower self that aspires to have "more" and "for longer".

The independent one is an egotistical being dependent on external factors that he selects according to his egotistical needs. He imposes limits and judgments towards factors that he judges as being too suffocating for his psychophysical fulfillment. These units become the prison within which he "evolves" without however becoming evolved. Through his independence he creates a false image of what a self-sufficient human being must be. Being self-sufficient is a question of autonomy more than of independence.

# The Ashram is not Autonomous

First of all, the ashram sees itself as independent, which it is, but it is far from being autonomous. Each member requires special attention from the Master, each one wanting to be part of the Master's intimate circle when everyone in a sense, already belongs.

You are that which constitutes the nature of the Master, but your action poisons his existence and prevents the expansion of your destiny. Your cry is for independence, you demand this independence instead of cultivating autonomy. You close yourself off to others by forgetting to open yourself up truly. The lower self guides each and every one of you and you are lead by your "desires" to be recognized and sentimentally loved by the Master. You discuss and doubt his affirmations and judgments; you desire more recognition and you cry for yourselves.

The Path of discipleship is not for the faint of heart and who among you can claim not to be? You clamour for your place within the group, but at what price? What do you give in exchange? Conditions, attachments? Reflect and stop complaining.

# Verify Your Innermost Motivations

I am not here to take pity on you or to criticize you, but to warn you about yourself and the effects that certain undesirable attitudes can engender.

You have the power to make the Ashram grow, but you also have the power to destroy it. I am aware of your doubts and of your questioning, but that only makes me more confident in human nature who knows how to recognize its mistakes and who continues on the right path.

Doubts do not have their place when you are under the guidance of a Master. Your questioning must not be directed towards him or his actions, but towards yourself and your motivations. If you cannot act with complete confidence towards your Master, we cannot do so towards you since you are not "responsible" for yourself because you make others responsible when in fact it is all up to you. How can you expect us to ask more of you as a disciple or as an Ashram when your interests are directed only towards yourself?

Illusion takes on many facets, especially on the path of discipleship and don't forget that tantrism makes everything surface, especially that which needs to be worked and purified. The thirst for power, for success and for control still very much influences your behaviour and your actions.

You are not attached to your Meditation Center or to its works, but to the comfort and the power that it gives you. Its disappearance would facilitate the work of the Master unless a spectacular change in your actions takes place. I repeat, tantrism is not for everyone and receiving such a teaching is a privilege that you seem to neglect. Does it make you too uncomfortable? Does this teaching bring out your lower aspects, such as your childish self, egotistical self or your insecurity?

These basic points that undermine your discipleship must be worked upon and withdrawn from your aura. This will require a lot of work on your part and only those who truly love their Master will succeed.

The love for the Master is essential and only this love can save you from yourself. I do not in any way cast doubt on the motivations of your Master who is my beloved disciple. If you doubt him, you also doubt me as well as the Ashram (Khutumi's Ashram) with which we are affiliated.

We have invested much in your Center, but your arrogance makes our task almost impossible to realize. You have the potential to succeed, but your attitude makes this task impossible for the moment. My words do not in any way invalidate my love for all of you. I simply ask that you undertake a profound examination of your consciousness and to above all verify your deepest motivations. Trust your Master, help him, love him and you will be rewarded. Not by flattery or by words that will inflate your ego, since your only true goal, if you are true disciples, isn't the worldly aspects related to the Ashram, but your sincere and deep desire to evolve.

Free your Master of your existential concerns, but above all of your illusions of grandeur, of your desire to be recognized, to be exceptional and unique. In our eyes, you are all "exceptional" in your way of being "ordinary"; an ordinariness that you must render extra-ordinary.

I have hope in you, because I have eternity. I am with you, I love you, but I am willing to wait so that an awakening can take place within the group. An awakening that, I hope, will occur soon. Your potential is still dormant. You are like Sleeping Beauty, you sleep and the dreams you have are of both suffering and illusion. Nothing is real, except my love for you and your Master.

When will you become "real" and "authentic" men and women? Never forget who your Master is, is it your ego or Master Etbonan Karta, my disciple? I am not enraged with you, I am furious that you force me to intervene. My time is more precious than you can believe and at the moment I doubt that my time is being used as it should be. Are you worth it? The future will tell. And on this note I take my leave of you and return to my task.

# Sexuality Within Tantrism

Tantrism isn't used to camouflage God, or if you prefer His Divinity, with practices that only serve to distract man's attention. Tantrism plunges man, because he is unaccustomed to contacting the soul, into deep work aimed at going beyond the ego, or if you prefer, to outsmart it, so that it will no longer hamper the journey of the sincere disciple who wishes to progress towards the Light of God, which is well beyond the soul and the Monad.

Tantrism is a small step towards the Divinity that is asleep within us, but it is a big step towards the conquest of that which keeps you prisoner of your own self. You must conquer your thoughts and your emotions, which have way too much influence in your lives.

The physical body has very little importance within authentic tantrism. It must not hinder, since it is but a base that you should have already worked on in past lives. You must not be a slave to your physical body and to its needs, even sexual. If this is the case, you are not ready for tantrism.

Those who use only sexuality as a means of tantric expression follow a false path, because they become more enslaved to their body, but above all to the ecstatic sensations that the body procures. You will not bring your body anywhere after your death, and that is what is different from your Mind, which is the true tantric vehicule. Flow towards it and within it and you will attain a plenitude that no sexual act, called tantric, can give you.

Do not be limited by matter. Respect it, love it, but be free of it. Free to express yourself through it, all the while being worthy of the Light that wishes to pass through you, in your soul and your Mind. We must not neglect the body, but one must above all put one's attention elsewhere. Raise your Mind and your body will be the better for it.

Sexuality has allowed the species to survive, but it also showed man that he is pure energy. However, even if it can demonstrate this energy, it is not this energy, because sexuality is mechanical. You confuse the content with the container. Sexual organs are useful as are our hands, skin and eyes, but they are not essential to your evolution. They are not the "heart" of your evolution. They are but a tool that you must use wisely.

Sexuality must not guide you and become your master. It is and must continue to be, a temporary learning tool and a tool for reproduction. It allows closeness, but that's where its impact resides; closer contact and not a goal towards union. Sexuality holds many secrets, but they cannot be revealed and understood except by those who have the energetic capacity to not submit to it, but who rather subdue it in order for it to be what it "is": a learning tool as are your emotions and your physical body.

Don't give sexuality more importance than it actually has. In left-handed tantrism, sexuality is used as a means of expression. Those who practice this do not realize that they are hindered by their exaggerated attachment to sex. Sex then is transformed into an extra weight added to the obstacles that litter their path.

Sexuality is an ally when it is used wisely, by respecting the Devas that are associated with it. The Devas associated with the sexual organs and the sexual act are not responsible for the Kundalini activation, as some believe. They are simply responsible for the culture of fire related to the sexual act.

To sublimate the sexual act and to render its fire more subtle, the intervention of tantric divinities known as Daikinis, is required. They possess other more appropriate names concerning their real work with the use of magic or etheric use of the sexual act. I won't say more because it would be too soon for the reader interested only in awakening through the sexual act by raising the Kundalini. Calling upon these Goddesses can bring destruction, since the fire of these divinities is so powerful they can render the one ill-prepared and ill-advised, instantly insane.

The wrong use and wrong understanding can create an even greater addiction for the world of sex, around which gravitate numerous demons that nourish themselves with this badly used energy and then redistribute it in gratuitous acts of violence towards the population that need not experience such criminal acts. These violent actions are a result of badly used and badly absorbed energy that is found captive in the Earth's atmosphere and spreads out everywhere that the negative telluric currents will take it. The negative sexual acts in Japan affect South Africa, those of Russia, Normandy and the East coast of the United States. Canada is affected by the negative energies emitted by Russia, but also by our English and French friends. We also affect them.

| | | |
|---|---|---|
| North Africa | $\xrightarrow{\text{affects}}$ | Scotland and Norway |
| Canada | → | Russia, Italy, England and a part of France |
| United States | → | Russia, Japan, and China |
| South America | → | Japan, Italy, Spain, and New Zealand |
| Australia | → | Philippines, Tahiti, Haiti, and New Zealnd |
| Greece | → | Italy, Eastern Europe and North Africa |
| Arab countries | → | United States (West coast), and North Africa |

# The Misuse of Sexuality

The wrong use of sexuality in terms of energy, affects the universal consciousness of man more than you think. Through the intermediary of the students and disciples, it can even affect the important task of the Master.

When the mind of a student is preoccupied by sexuality and the related modes of expression, he affects, via his aura, the aura of the group to which he belongs. The student thus also affects the aura of the Master since he carries the entire group in his bosom, and therefore the aura of the group that little by little perturbs the Master's work.

Sexual abstinence is not the solution since that brings with it major energy deficiencies regarding certain nadis and chakras that are essential for the evolution of human consciousness. However, certain lives of abstinence or certain parts of one's life lived in abstinence may be necessary if there has been abuse of sexuality in past lives.

The parts of life in which sexuality diminishes its activity and domination on man's psyche, allows for a profound cleansing of the nadis that have been "infected" by the excess of misused sexuality. Man then begins to exercise a beneficial "control" on his life through the adequate use of sexuality.

Every being on the planet is sexual, but every being must dominate this force that drives man's desire, subjugated by the magnetism that sexuality exerts, therefore experiencing and forcing others to experience abuses of this energy. This implies an increasingly erroneous alignment with man's true consciousness.

One must understand the mechanism of sexuality at a very deep level before mastering it in the positive or negative sense. Black magicians master this art perfectly and use it to dominate and control not only consciousness but the soul as well, which becomes impure with pestilent vapors emitted due to misused sexuality as it is used for egotistical purposes.

Such a damaged soul must then be cleansed by these influences and the most efficient method of doing so continues to be the isolation of the soul from this energy. This isolation can be done under the guidance of a Master who will allow the individual to experience a greater passion than that of sexuality. The exchange of these forces allows the individual to free himself little by little from the hold that a misunderstood and wrongly used sexuality has on him. This will take months, years and sometimes lifetimes before the harmful effects of misused sexuality can disappear. It will then be up to the individual to learn the sexual game once again, but in an appropriate and healthy way.

Sexuality is a complex art that can facilitate an individual's progress or drive him into hells that are difficult to get out of. Be alert and pay attention. The danger persists even if you believe you are immune to this harmful negative state that is linked to the negative abuse of sexuality.

# Growing Through Sexuality

Tantrism allows those who have it in their hearts to evolve, to better understand the sexual games that increase to the extent that an understanding is correctly adjusted. When I mention "growing" I am referring to the divine aspect related to sexuality.

Growing in one's sexuality is more complex than you can imagine since every living being is "sexual" and transforms himself through the sexual game. This complex game, which can imprison us, can also drive energy to specific areas of the body, allowing light to get to these areas and to effect specific work linked to our Higher Self.

When you are advanced on the path, a sexual partner can be optional since sexual energy flows freely in the body of the initiate without encountering any obstacles. The human orgasm allows certain psychic barriers to fall, barriers that prevent the individual to bypass the mental, and to therefore attain a supra-mental energy that is difficult to come by, by any other means. The orgasm allows the temporary forgetting of one's self thus allowing access to the luminous platform situated in the pineal gland where everything becomes possible.

From this focal access point, the energy can be directed in different directions and produce lasting effects. The achievement of this first focal point takes place at the 3rd initiation in which there is often a temporarily reduced libido. The effect of this is to lead the initiate to cultivate this latent sexual energy on his own in order to allow it to freely cross over the borders and obstacles issuing from the mental. At this stage, the sexual act becomes secondary, but is still necessary for procreation and for emotional bonding.

Such a being appears to be "asexual" from the outside perspective, but in fact isn't, and this isn't easily understood. He will only too often be categorized as abnormal by his equals or treated as someone who is "stuck" by those who cannot "see". For this reason initiates will from now on, get married and have children up until their tasks are accomplished among humans. This means that a 6th or 7th level initiate will experience a sexuality that appears normal even though, their circuitry being perfect, sexuality will no longer be a need but be a shared joy without expectations.

# Understanding Sexuality

There will never be enough talk on the subject of sexuality since it is now being misused and misunderstood. Its energetic impact can influence man positively or negatively on his evolutionary path.

It has already been mistakenly mentioned in certain texts that wrongly used sexuality creates what we call the tail of the devil, in the etheric field. Claiming that it had an inverse circulation, it was projected, etherically speaking, from the physical body from its central point located at the base of the spine, which apparently produced this diabolic tail. Nothing could be further from the truth.

The misuse of sexuality, the abuse and excesses created by its energy produces important blockages preventing man from seeing the Light, his own Light, which causes him intolerable suffering that he attempts to forget through this abusive sexuality. The worse poison for man is his erroneous concepts that he has towards himself and towards that which animates him.

Man is a magician of words, thanks to his lower mind that is too often influenced by involuted forces that wish to keep him prisoner of his old concepts that prevent him from evolving and growing in the Light. Man must be educated and raised to the rank that suits him, but obstacles created by the prolific lower mind render the task extremely arduous for the Masters who tirelessly attempt to awaken his consciousness so that the Light of the soul and of the Monad can circulate freely within him.

Humanity is suffering and this suffering is generated in large part by the incomprehension of certain laws. One of these laws is the Law of Constancy. This means being constant in that which the soul tries desperately to learn and to communicate to us.

When the soul will have completed its learning, it will be reabsorbed into the Monad and its destiny will have been accomplished. However due to man's egoic[2] personality that prevents him from being constant in his apprenticeship, the soul's task is painful and difficult. This creates unnecessary suffering that is added to the suffering that already exists in a personality that is resistant to change.

---

[2] Refers to the ego.

# Man's Unconsciousness

Without tantrism, which is what in reality animates all animated things, man would not grow and become the potential divine being that is asleep on the sparkling eyelash of the one we like to call God, a God that is beyond concepts, beyond norms and human laws that now plague our planet and poison it.

Some good souls with goodwill attempt to rebalance, without success, the precarious balance that prevents man from sinking completely in the pit of his ignorance and above all his unconsciousness. Man cheerfully handles the art of not becoming aware in such a way that he denies the existence of the disturbances that he causes here and elsewhere.

Man's unconsciousness not only disturbs the evolved beings on this planet and the influential members of the different ashrams, but also perturbs the peace of mind of living beings in other systems than ours.

Through his infantile behaviour, man is centered on himself in such a way that he is voluntarily ignored by beings of deep wisdom who hope and wait with patience for the awakening of man and especially for the reduction of his mental and emotional arrogance.

Man is a proud being, but when this aspect is abused, it can quickly become pride that easily transforms into arrogance that taints each thought, each action, each event brought on by man's ineptness, who seeks power instead of wisdom. The wise person knows that he is master of himself and of that which animates him. He has the power, since all wise beings are beings of power, whereas not all men of power are necessarily wise, and I would even say that they are rarely so.

# Solitude Through Tantrism

The time at hand is about change at all levels and tantrism acts in proportion to the individual's desire for change. Tantrism respects that which is respectable and does not respect that which is not. It tramples on antiquated and useless principles and attracts to itself or through it that which is necessary to accomplish the task of man or woman who is evolving solitarily and solidarily on the path.

Through tantrism, man feels at his deepest level a solitude that only he can understand and experience. He can share his experiences with his brothers on the path, but only he experiences it, as his brothers experience their own solitude.

The exchanges among those who progress on the path cannot attenuate this solitude just as they cannot increase it. No, those exchanges are not meant to heal or diminish the pain of solitude, but to support and encourage the disciple's constant efforts towards the progression of his destiny.

Many use sexuality as recourse to forget the emptiness that they cover up with solitude, others throw themselves into work or the dizziness of everyday life. The idiots consume more and the so-called unavoidable New Age evolution teaches auto-sufficiency and the means to effectively escape this painful emptiness in which solitude works out its transformational goal. Even after "the discovery" of "we are never alone", solitude persists, more present but also more nourishing.

It allows man to fulfill himself while accomplishing more. One must not flee from solitude, but cultivate it adequately in order that it becomes a sure ally on the road of transformation. Tantrism favors solitude, since through it many things can be accomplished. The good man cannot manage anything without it, since it is the spice that allows ideas to burst forth outside of his consciousness, a consciousness that is no longer perturbed by distractions that only cause him to be further removed from the goal that we wish to attain.

All is effort in this world and ignoring it puts us in grave danger and above all makes us waste precious time. The evolution on this planet will be slow as long as man does not accept to leave behind the useless comfort that destroys the human will. A comfort that doesn't contribute to evolution is as harmful to the soul as is a virulent poison to the health of the body. One must subdue comfort and not become dependent or attached to it.

# Attachment and Autonomy

Attachment can create numerous obstacles to evolution especially when it is misunderstood and badly used, since attachment causes dependency and kills autonomy. What is needed is a healthy attachment that allows for the expansion of consciousness and not its contraction.

Detachment is also misunderstood and it is a deception because detachment does not exist; only a healthy attachment allows growth and unfoldment in this universe in which everything is linked and in some ways dependent or autonomous according to the vision we have and how we experience it.

Being attached is fine as long as we remain autonomous. Being detached and independent is an illusion that has nothing to do with the Realization of our highest potential and this false perception further links us to the human condition.

When truly understood, the positive pole of attachment can lead man to accomplish great things since through attachment he can become part of the Universe where his design becomes reality of that which manifests him. Experiencing one's design in a healthy way implies a willing attachment to the design that is our due since without this subtle link nothing can be accomplished; everything needs to be started over again.

Sincere detachment exists only in fairy tales where the hero is just a puppet among other puppets. He believes he is detached, but invisible threads keep him tied to what he believes is his destiny when in fact he is destiny's game, which has nothing to do with his own destiny. The puppet strings are activated by what he thinks is correct according to his erroneous vision, when instead true spiritual growth implies a strong attachment, but autonomous without expectations of return.

Understanding attachment in its positive sense can lead to enormous realizations. Without attachment, man is condemned to err in the maze of illusions that further complicates his existence.

Everyone has many attachments, more or less subtle, which facilitate or impede his evolution. A being without attachments cannot exist on this planet nor in this universe since all is related by etheric threads that make interdimensional communication possible.

No substances would exist since no molecule could attach itself and create the Law of Attraction that allows the atom to be what it is. Attraction engenders attachment, but attraction cannot exist without the consequence of attachment. One is the result of the other and we call this the Law of Cause and Effect. Attachment also creates attraction thus creating a communication without end between what attracts and what is attracted. The Law of Attraction is as essential as the Law of Attachment, allowing matter to be what it is, since without these Laws neither visible nor invisible matter could exist. The fear of attachment comes from the fear of commitment and from the fear of taking on one's destiny. We believe we are subject to our destiny whereas it is created and conforms to what we profoundly desire according to our soul.

# Tantrism Cannot be Understood Logically

There exist many paths and roads within tantrism that allow the individual to accede more or less rapidly towards the apogee of his terrestrial existence. This is why tantrism goes beyond the soul and all that this implies concerning earthly life.

Authentic tantrism, the one that allows man to become his own master and master of his destiny, cannot manifest itself through the physical brain. It can only imbue it with its energy and be understood by the higher Mind, which is directly linked to the lower Monad, which by far surpasses the energy manifested by the higher level of the soul.

All is understood and complete when the manifestation of the perception of God, through matter, is completed in the human kingdom by the human himself.

The liberation of humanity must go through steps of liberation within man's individual consciousness, which is conveyed through the earthly manifestation of matter.

No freedom is authentic as long as man hasn't attained this stage where all manifestation becomes possible via a human consciousness that is purified of imperfections stemming from the materialization of God's thought via this illusory world that represents the world of form. The thought of God is crystallized only by and in the human mind that uses it for the goal of apprenticeship and for the knowledge of good and evil. These two polarities only have their existence by virtue of what we call the manifestation current of that which is divine and what flows from this. Understanding the power of good and evil means understanding the origin of form manifested through the thought of God, engendered in a world beyond form.

# Doubt

Via that which we call tantrism, man circulates first of all within him, doubt, which represents his dark side. He <u>doubts</u> everything, except himself, in order to one day arrive at the realization that the only thing he must doubt is in fact himself since everything that is happening to him has been foreseen and requested by his soul.

When man realizes this at a profound level, he also realizes that doubt only exists in order to allow him to question himself and nothing else. Nothing is served by doubting that which surrounds him and especially those who surround him. He alone is responsible for his progress but above all for his unhappiness that he attributes only too easily to others, especially his loved ones.

No one doubts that following the path of tantrism leads one to assimilate within oneself the advantages and disadvantages — the "for and against"— of the evolution that continues on despite the obstacles. We all benefit in pursuing this path, since the "for" (advantages) that stem co-jointly from the soul and the Monad support humanity's design in regards to what it came here to experience and to create.

On the whole, evolution leads to the positive side of human life within the concept emitted by God or that which we call the Inconceivable. The "against" (disadvantages) that consider evolution from the point of view of the mortal soul, are in fact nothing but astral projections that create the inevitable obstacles that we must confront. Going beyond these obstacles frightens us, but the suffering that this engenders scares us even more. Of course, if evolution could be had only through the love and comfort of the Divine, there would exist only the "for" evolution, but alas this is not the case and in order to de-crystallize himself man must go through the fire of purification that unearths the enemies of evolution along its way.

# Acceptance

Secondly, through tantrism, man must allow <u>acceptance</u> for everything that occurs to him and that will occur to him, to flow through him, despite his fear of change and of evolving. Evolving hurts as long as acceptance is not integrated and practiced daily.

As long as man doubts, it will be impossible for him to accept the path of service, which results in the constant forgetting of one's self. This can be disturbing to those who observe with profane eyes since he only sees the external and ignores everything that is truly going on at man's deepest levels.

When acceptance is experienced without obstacle, man then undertakes the path of return that implies a constant forgetting of self, accompanied by a clear and just vision for the mission to be accomplished, for himself and for humanity. He becomes the knight without fear of the destiny of the human Hierarchy beyond the physical worlds and the parallel worlds that this implies. What is relative is constant via the inevitability of that which will be produced and will occur in order to complete the circle of human evolution.

# Inconstancy

Thirdly, via tantrism, man must allow the circulation of the <u>inconstancy</u> of all that is to flow through him. All is movement, all is change. No second that passes is the same as the following one or the preceding one, each second being unique and universal and can't be compared one to the other because all together they shape all that is just and that which must be accomplished and realized. Life flows with movement; without movement life becomes static.

# Tantrism is Unique and not Buddhic

Tantrism must not be understood within the context of Buddhism. Although Buddhism has helped to make tantrism known, tantrism is a separate and autonomous entity. It fluctuates according to its own rhythm and is not influenced by any factors associated with a philosophy or a religion.

It is unique, as we are, but untameable and incomprehensible to the one who tries to define it as an entity that is conditional and limited to certain factors. Nothing really influences tantrism, except tantrism itself, which evolves according to the era and the people to whom it addresses itself. It is not subject to fixed and rigid laws, but respects the one who is noble at heart and who sincerely progresses upon the path.

Respect tantrism in all its power and splendour and it will respect you. Do not respect it and it will destroy you or neutralize you in the areas that are most dear to you. Do not take it lightly and don't underestimate it. It is what it is within that which is the most powerful and elevating in terms of vibrational energy, stimulating Mind for the conquest of the inter-dimensional and multi-dimensional Universe to which he belongs.

# Consciousness

The unfathomable cannot be known and cannot therefore be explained in clear language. It can only be felt and integrated via different paths that have nothing in common with the concrete mind, a mind that needs to be bypassed in order to allow the energy to flow freely through the circuits binding the soul as an evolutionary entity of the Monad who will become its guide and its goal.

The energy that is born becomes condensed and then circulates via the channels of the conscious being; it accumulates thanks to a strict discipline from a consciousness that has been vivified by the silence of the being who condenses and purifies it. Consciousness with a capital "C" must become the occult cauldron for that which must be known in terms of absence of doubt towards that which "is" and that which will "become" a memorable moment of the perfect moment of the present that contains both the past and the future of what should be and of that which we are in our energetic potential as conscious beings.

It is useless to cultivate the lower consciousness because it will become a prison for that which must be expressed. The lower consciousness must be "educated" in order for it to become the perfect partner of that which must evolve through man. Man is made up of the concrete mind linked to the lower consciousness, which in turn has a close link with morality that imposes certain evolutionary and inconstant conditions.

Moral standards can change according to the needs of the people and of the Rays that govern them. Morality cannot evolve because it is a synthetic process created in order to allow man to experiment further the different ranges of the personality played out according to the physical needs of the different incarnations experienced on this planet. Morality can be transcended but not destroyed since its constancy assures a certain equilibrium for human ecology. Were it not for the injection of morality to satisfy this constancy, human beings would have ceased to exist a long time ago. Morality stabilizes those who have a need for it in order to perfect a certain degree of perfection.

Morality partly rules the lower consciousness, which in turn influences concrete mind. We wrongly believe that it is the concrete mind that conditions the lower consciousness. Concrete mind can be cultivated via external information. Consciousness arises from a constant repetition of experiences, lessons and acquired sufferings during incarnations. It is a stable reservoir of that which we have experienced since our creation as human beings. Sometimes consciousness allows itself to be influenced by morality that taints it temporarily because of the need for lessons that the lower consciousness must acquire during a specific incarnation.

# Don't Let Doubt Get You!

Never doubt yourself as spirit, because doubting creates an energetic field conducive to what we call the involutive aspect of that which has been created to grow and not the inverse. Tantrism can create the illusion of doubt, since doubt must be eliminated or dissolved in its positive aspect for the individual who is transforming.

# The Goal in Creating Man

Man was created with the goal of accomplishing a specific design desired by that which we commonly call "God" or "The One That Is". In this design, God, as a pure and true Light entity, established certain bases or difficulties allowing man to travel the breadth and depth of the maze of some dark aspects that were not at the time accessible to the eye of God. And so, in order to help man return to the Light, the soul was created in the hopes that this Ariane's thread would lead him back to the source of that which expresses the Intelligence of God.

The soul, which was not that effective in the beginning, had to perfect its nature in order to intensify its own Light, which at that time was nothing but a small dot without much luminescence. During the incarnations experienced by all of humanity, the soul or souls learned how to condense and purify their own Light so as to become more attractive to the gaze of man's personality, which until then was only attracted to that which the world of matter radiated.

The human personality became aware of a Light that was purer and more direct and it took pleasure in turning towards it in order to contemplate the splendor that allowed the personality to covet something more perfect and more grandiose than itself. The soul grew in Light while the personality grew in wisdom. In order for the possibility of fusion to become possible, both had to work hard at submission: the soul had to submit to God's design via its guide the Monad, and the personality had to submit to the Will of God via the soul, now its guide. ·

The exploration continues because the soul is only at the beginning of its functions. It still hasn't completed its work and must further perfect its vision and refine its actions, in order to allow a much greater humanity to be birthed within that which it expresses.

The complaints and the self-pity only serve to make the progress towards change more difficult. Man must learn to turn towards his higher Self that will become the seed of his authentic nature. From this seed will grow all of his erudition, his wisdom, right speech, right action and right seeing.

The intensity towards the expression of his true nature will become possible and will be a Divine right that is his due. His doubt towards his own realization has created a doubt about the realization of God's own goal. Nothing can be accomplished without a radical transformation of that which man presently expresses. Man's confusion comes from his lack of wisdom based on an erroneous vision of what he believes is real and acceptable for his survival.

Man does not believe that he is immortal; he believes he is vulnerable and hides his despair by externalizing the superficial aspects of his life. He creates the glamour of the physical, the word and thought, which are nothing but pale and meager reflections of that which God expresses via the manifestation of his molecular expression, but above all, cellular expression.

# The Extinction of Humanity

Man's vision must change. Without a mutation of the involutive thinking of the human kingdom, its extinction is imminent. A reprieve of 100,000 years has been given to mankind in order to grant him a Divine state that is more appropriate to his destiny. If this state is not attained, the terrestrial experience will end and the souls will be sent to other systems where the freedom of "being" will be less prominent.

A tight framework must be available in order to "educate" those souls lost in the maze of their overly strong personality. Man must "tame" the ego, because it is the cause of his imminent demise. 100,000 years, that's all, since it represents between 20 to 50 lives for the majority of people because man will live longer but not necessarily with more wisdom. In about 500 years the average life span will reach about 190 years and another 100 years will be added on quickly. Man will easily live to be 500 years old 5000 years from now, but at what price? He will have other temptations that will increase his unconsciousness. If wisdom doesn't take its place, destruction will occur and no reprieve will be allowed.

Man is not immortal as a thinking being living on this planet, which he too often scorns. Man's destiny is precarious as long as he doesn't integrate and accept that he is merely the result of what he believes himself to be.

Changing this perspective will change everything. Destabilize man's center and an enormous potential will open up for him, since it is only in that unstable and precarious moment that a Divine spark of understanding can surface within him.

As long as he remains stable, man cannot change because he cannot be shaken up within his structure. This spark that we define as Divine is in fact the transmutation of lead into gold, that is to say, the electrical transmutation of a precise point inside the brain that directly affects the vibratory system of thought. First there is an impact on the etheric level, but the real change only occurs when there is a result on the equivalent physical point, which is related to the concrete thought of the subject who cannot but obey and change attitude.

The lightening bolt happens via a chemical exchange in a brain cell affected by a sudden descent of energy issuing from an opening in the etheric body created by "Divine" or "Atmic" manifestation that influences the atom, which enflames itself with a sap, produced by the friction of this light and the dense physical of the individual. There is a gaseous exchange and an electro-atomic change ensues creating multiple perturbations within the individual, which then creates a chain reaction of inner changes that disrupts each cell of the individual subjected to this fate.

A good attitude during the impact will lead to a temporary victory for the Self (lower or higher Self depending on the individual's degree of evolution), whereas a negative attitude will lead to a momentary loss of the individual's spiritual path and he will be overwhelmed by negative emotions that will create a thick fog upon his consciousness and will distort his vision. He will become the pawn of the ego, now even stronger and more destructive.

# The Process of Rejuvenation

The process of rejuvenation is related to tantrism only from the cellular perspective. One has to bypass the conscious level in order to touch the central point conveying fictitious data about the future. One must admit that all is not written, especially from the point of view of human genetics.

Thought can destroy, but it cannot effectively construct a process on the long term. It can put down foundations, but it will be incapable of building walls, because this is the task of another process that is not physical, since it is not temporal.

We must look to the atom that is energetically responsible for the anchoring point of time, both past and future. Time can cease its influence while allowing the future to take its place without creating any repercussions or damage to the physical cells. Do not use thought, use the vibration of sound, which connects with the intelligence of Higher Mind in order to diffuse that which is in gear and must occur in terms of the chain of evolution of humanity.

It is possible to break this chain reaction and to be removed from this repetitive cycle. Many have done so and their secret, which is so well guarded asks nothing but to be revealed to those who can listen beyond the principle of a precise moment of the present, straddling upon an inexistent time within the concreteness of a Divine Reality.

# Eternal Youth

Make space inside yourself and you will learn to read within the formless that conceals the secret of eternal physical youth. The duality of form, as it now exists, must disappear and dissolve into that which we commonly call the duality of what exists across the unique existence of that which cannot be known in terms of mortal and destructible terrestrial form.

The dimension of that which exists in you as an immortal individual, must take its birth in the tiniest part of yourself, which we consider the most powerful since it has not been tainted by the mortal aspect of your experiences. The secret resides within you and not in the sophisticated techniques that dull consciousness while attempting to liberate the physical body.

You will experience the immensity that can be experienced within the immortality of that which exists. Death is a deception and old age even more so. Break the mirage and go beyond the illusion of form that only exists because of your desire for this existence.

# Duality

As long as there is life on earth, there will be duality because of the planetary influence. This planet is one of duality, therefore everything that lives on it, is also dual, since everything is subject to this Law. There is the day, and there is the night, there is good and there is evil. These are all different concepts, but derived from the same source.

This source influences everything, even if it is not of this world. It commands energy, which in turn influences both subtle and dense matter. This source, which isn't God itself, was born at the confines of what we call the waking dream of God. If this source is understood, it can help conquer the duality of life, death, youth and old age. It is therefore found there where nothing else exists except its own existence, which is neither real nor fiction.

This source can free up energy that goes beyond the concepts related to this planet. It makes the Mind free of all earthly attachments, since conquering the principle of duality implies the conquest of that which exists beyond this duality and makes man a cosmic being instead of a universal being. Man defines himself through principles that help him to conserve his form. In order to go beyond these principles, we have to have the uncommon strength of someone who can be bonded without attachments. We have to ignore the emptiness and not be subject to it, or else there will be absorption of the form instead of its liberation.

The principle of non-duality was founded by a spirit trying to escape the karmic law related to this planet. We cannot escape duality; we can only navigate through it. This principle of duality is life and the concept of life. It allows the insertion of cycles precious to the unfoldment of the human soul. Through duality the soul learns how to combat the imbalance of that which is not in harmony with comings and goings of that which characterizes us here. We find our strength through this battle that obliges us to face up to the Divine principle that implies that everything is fair even in the negativity of things.

The comings and goings of earthly life meets up very well with what is the soul's most precious learning: the equilibrium point of non-existence, which seems to characterize us. We are a deception for the soul's perception, a useful deception and necessary in its role. The soul must define itself beyond the law of earthly attraction that overlaps with many concepts that are limiting to its true expression. The soul isn't dualistic, it is its expression through matter that is. The soul is not unique, it is multiple in the veracity of its source. It is not immortal, nor real; it is an expression of what must temporarily exist in this space-time linked to its existence. It is but the diluted expression of a principle to which it is subject, since it is an integral part of the God principle via the Monadic function, which it too, is under the dualistic influence of the human existence, since the Monad qualifies the soul which in turn qualifies the human aspect of the realized being.

# The Monad

Contrary to the soul, the Monad was never created. It "is" a direct descendant of that which we call the Intelligent aspect of God. This aspect allows the sensitive person to turn towards this divine energy of just compassion, which when integrated can make him not "universal" but multi-dimensional. He can then go from one plane of consciousness to another without however being affected by the consciousness of that level. The Monad has this Divine quality of understanding within his bosom, which allows man to realize himself in his true destiny that isn't part of this dimension called "Earth" or "dense matter".

The Monad is smaller than the atom, and smaller than the energy emitted by the atom. Despite this tiny aspect, its strength surpasses by far anything that can be known in terms of manifested space. These vibrations that we refer to as Monadic and not atomic have repercussions in spheres of activity unattainable by human thought.

The Monad must not be understood with the mind, since understanding it in this manner greatly diminishes its role within the Mind of man. The Monad, which can in no way be subjected, must be experienced before being understood intuitively and more directly than through the concrete mind.

# The Ether

Because of tantrism, man naively believes he can meet the origin of his source, whereas he needs to get to know his own source above all else. Tantrism guides man through the mazes of illusions that characterize his life. Man must go beyond that which he believes he his, by going directly from his subtle energy, which he has learned about and mastered, to another energy that is much more dynamic than his vibrational rate will ever be under the etheric aspect of his existence.

The Ether is fluid, light, filled with Light that sometimes, as with the astral plane, can present traps that keep man's spirit attached to this plane and blinded so that he can't follow his path. The Ether is animated by a force that has a double role. Its energy attracts and holds prisoner those who do not have the knowledge and wisdom of this world of which it is the guardian. With its invisible and luminous threads, it prevents all individuals who are not mature enough, to reach a plane of consciousness that would allow them a degree of inexplicable perfection. This perfection is possible because of an energy field that encloses the secrets of that which cannot be understood with concrete intelligence and via the Higher Mind, which is just a necessary landing used for the achievement of this state.

# Perfection

The state that we consider "Nirvana", which is often confused with this plane whereas it is one level higher, allows the atom that is the essence of man to go to a state where the speed of light becomes his mental coat. He can do anything at all times, because he knows everything about this world and now knows about the reverse aspect of this world.

Matter is but a glove that hides this powerful hand that indicates the direction of this source, which goes beyond the concept we have of God. This hand, which shows the direction, cannot however guide one; it is but the intermediary of that which is and that which must be discovered. It is only the great of this world who have access, since this hidden aspect demands a perfect forgetfulness of our condition, in order that the Divine Plan can become accessible. These individuals are physically immortal, since they have been able to attain this state within themselves where time has no influence, since time is directed by mind (lower and higher mind). An "enlightened" individual remains physically mortal, since he has not yet attained this state of almost ultimate perfection.

# The Kirpan Aspect

The Kirpan aspect, derived from a Hebrew term, refers to the aspect of the Divine that cannot be understood via the mental, be it concrete mental or higher Mind. This aspect also refers to the state of dynamic beatitude that animates all that is continuous within the Verb aspect of God. It concerns tangible manifestation of that which must exist in its essence. It does not refer to matter, or to that which makes up matter. It refers to its attribute. It qualifies that which cannot be qualified and renders it accessible to the lower planes, of which the Monad and the Atman are a part.

When we combine the Kirpan with the Nirvana as tangible manifestation of this plane, we are not insinuating a platonic association. The Kirpan as well as the Nirvana follow positive states of the Verb aspect, and therefore of the creation of Divine nature. Attaining Nirvana has nothing romantic or mysterious about it. When man's Mind, which we also refer to as the Monad, turns towards the creator of which he is intimately a part, he perceives the shadow of his image and this leads him to a temporary error. He qualifies what he sees according to what he believes to be seeing when it is nothing but shade and shadows. He cannot clearly distinguish this new state, which he confuses with himself. He feels that it is a superior force, but doesn't dare approach it seriously. He is afraid of his reflection when the truth contained in Reality of that which "is" is something altogether different.

The Kirpan, in its most secretive aspect, cannot be recognized. It can only be felt through the very essence of that which constitutes it. The fabric to which it is linked is neither etheric nor mental. It is Nirvanic in the sense that it shines without brilliance and only depends on "sound", which makes it vibrate. Behind this sound, the Kirpan aspect manifests itself as a vibration carrying a sweet and joyous note of the Divine in its manifestation. The Kingdom of God is therefore very close to sounding in man's ear as a melodious note where all kingdoms and systems are confounded. Only this note resounds and now indicates the path of return in a clear fashion, less shadowy.

This plane is accessible to anyone who has acquired true wisdom of that which must be known as the manifestation of that which vibrates in the heart of the one who is beyond all physical vibrations. Wanting to attain this plane without having acquired this wisdom through difficulties and roadblocks on the path would be too great a risk for the equilibrium of the lower planes of which man is a part. An access that is too quick can cause irreparable damages, damages that then become obstacles to the changing of consciousness.

One must never underestimate the vibrational quality of that which vibrates at a higher level than ours. The intense period of becoming accustomed to this energy is of capital importance and crucial. Without a solid base, man's Spirit is at great risk. There will be no destruction, but a deceleration of the speed of growth for such an individual. A deceleration that will come close to the point of "no friction", with all luminous sparks becoming difficult to perceive and to see.

The Kirpan plane is that of clear adjustment of the system that manages the phenomenal world of thought. It is beyond Mind, beyond that which stimulates Mind and makes it efficient. The Kirpan plane has but only one goal, that of building this powerful energetic matrix that will confer without cease creative energetic waves of Divine order, from the point of view of sound, primordial instigator of everything that manages form. Without sound there is no form, since all molecules of matter vibrate to sound; it is what gives them life and movement, this also creates the Law of Attraction necessary to the movement of that which is animate. Thus the importance of music that allows matter to adjust to vibrations directly proportionate to those transmitted through music. The more the music elevates, the more consciousness follows suit. Music is the springboard that subtly guides the energy fields towards higher summits.

# The Planes

When we refer to "the planes" we are referring to that which we commonly refer to as the levels at which consciousness evolves. These planes are non-existant as long as consciousness does not qualify them as lived experiences through a reality that becomes concrete.

These levels are vibrational and resonate perfect notes, allowing the experimenting consciousness to convey and to express itself in a manner that is correct in regards to that which it is experimenting. These planes that we qualify as "inner", since they are linked to consciousness, are in reality beyond man's consciousness. They are independent and have no resonance to the call of consciousness, which cannot influence them. These planes are part of the Divine Matrix, accessible through atomic states of consciousness. The atom is related to everything that has form, even if this form appears invisible to us. Consciousness is raised when the atomic vibratory note resonates and adjusts itself to the Plane's perfect note, which welcomes into its bosom, the resonance of the consciousness that can now know and be known by the plane or level where consciousness can evolve. This aspect is not mysterious or miraculous; it is "technical".

# The Illusion of Tantra

When we undertake the path leading to the Realization of that which we believe we are, we are but at the first illusion that needs to be dissolved. Tantra is part of these illusions that are necessary, since tantra leads the individual to the conquest of the ego in order to subject it to the influence of the soul, which in turn must be conquered and subjected to the Law of the Monad.

In its manifestation, tantrism implies the existence of the soul as a supreme goal and ignores the presence of the Monad as God made manifest in the world of matter. Tantra leads us to the door where we can access the plane in which the Monad rules and stops at this point because tantra has cause or effect on only the lower subtle planes. It has no effect on the planes that go beyond the plane in which the Monad rules. Believing that tantrism can lead beyond the beyond leads to the supreme illusion that this technique, which in fact is not a technique, can do anything. This is false. It can make man God but not Divine in his totality. It partially illuminates man who will have to abandon it when the time will come for him to perfect his Divine role beyond that which seems to be known.

Padmasambhava knew these things and his teachings go far beyond what has been taught to man in regards to the path he has to undertake to perfect his perfection. He knew that even if he introduced this technique, it would one day become a ball and chain. Man, who has not yet arrived at this point, must conform himself to tantrism, but when the Monad plays Its first card, he must discard the game he will have learned, including tantrism.

# The Difficulty with Tantra

The difficulty with tantra is its non-conformity to existing rules. It can adapt to everything while retaining its stability. Practice emptiness and you will become empty. Practice fullness and you become full. Tantra favors neither one nor the other. It is the middle path. It allows one to perceive that which needs to be perceived all the while keeping hidden that which needs to be so. Revealing certain secrets too quickly can lead to the irreparable loss of certain energetic circuits. One must have the right dose and force nothing.

With tantrism, man rediscovers his true nature all the while focusing on that which characterizes him as man. He must define himself as such, before attempting to experiment something greater. Tantra is the boat that allows one to travel from one world to another in complete security if we are prudent. If it isn't the case, then the boat sinks as do we.

It is the same thing with an authentic Master who will know how to guide you from one shore to the other. Ignore this fact and you will sink instead of swim towards other lands more appropriate to your nature. Emptiness can only be realized if we accept that we are full of ourselves and of our expectations. Emptiness can only manifest through fine threads of this supreme truth that indicates that man, as he belongs to this world of matter, forgets that he is nothing but an atom seeking to express his supreme Divinity through his Light.

# The Right Understanding of Tantrism

Trying to understand what Spirit attempts to teach us is sometimes arduous, since its energy shakes up our schemas of thought and shatters our concepts of life. The opening that creates a good understanding of tantrism in its totality can allow the energy of the soul to ally itself with the higher Mind in order to allow us to more adequately receive what our ancestors called Divine knowledge of all that ever was through the intrinsic nature of that which exists.

The Spirit of man is but a segment of the immensity that is within him. Man, in his totality is much more than that once he succeeds in detaching himself from the lower mind and the conceptual non-world that makes him a slave to the non-essential needs of his existence.

The need that man has to reflect comes from his desire to grow in the world that he himself shapes from grandiose hopes related to his personality. When man will learn to detach himself from this conceptual mode and plunge happily into a world directed by an Intuition worthy to be revealed through him, he will finally know his glory and will perceive the true Goal of his existence.

Understanding the existence of the higher planes will not lead to the liberation of man's mind. On the contrary, it can make it more of a slave to concepts. Man must integrate within himself the energy that lives within him as soul and as Mind of his own Revelation.

Tantrism cannot reveal to man that which he really is. It can but show the path and point in the direction in which the personality will become a tool allowing the perfecting of man's destiny by liberating him from its influence and by leading him to the higher planes of his form that is no longer physical, but highly etheric.

Tantrism isn't a mode of sexual, mental or devotional expression. It is the perfect listening of the path that is essential to the maintenance of stability of that which wishes to freely express itself through man who is liberated from the world of existential form of which he believes to be dependent. The liberation that produces the perfect use of tantrism in its material non-existence, allows man to propel himself towards the authentic and Monadic aspects of himself.

Tantrism titillates the inclusive aspect of the soul, but its real task is to attain the Monadic energy and to insert it into that which we consider to be the source and the starting point of that which leads man to incarnate himself in this earthly dimension.

Man could have chosen more comfortable lives in more hospitable universes or dimensions. But such was not the case because his bold spirit has always been attracted to the occult aspect that encloses the world of form, and in order to get to know this aspect he had no choice but to plunge into it.

In actuality, it isn't the soul that chooses the incarnation, it is man's Spirit that guides him in his choice. Spirit has neither concept nor dress as the soul does. Spirit is but energy that expresses itself according to the rhythm of that which needs to be expressed so that, that which characterizes it can decrease its vibrational rate and diminish its frequency thus allowing the phenomenal world to express itself through him. Spirit cannot tame matter, it can but attempt to understand it in order to respect its Laws, which can then be changed and transformed since they are not necessary to the accomplishment plishment of the Plan.

The link between Spirit and matter is an important occult link, since through it is expressed God's Plan, who wishes to know His work in the smallest details. The sacrifice of the soul, but mostly of the Spirit, makes it such that when man will have completed his apprenticeship here, that which we call God, he will have accomplished an infinite part of his Destiny that is without end.

Man, or rather the Spirit of man collaborates with the Beauty of God in the sense that it activates the perfection of God in a totality of complex and unlimited data. We cannot understand, but observing such a phenomena can lead to that which man's Spirit aspires, that is to say its Divine nature that seeks to express itself in that which is the most pure within that which is the most dense in the worlds that characterize the Divine Spirit.

# Epilogue

We would not know how to define tantrism in concrete and easily understood terms, since this would demystify one of the greatest occult mysteries concerning one of the paths that leads man to his perfection. Tantrism must remain energy, mystery and experience in order to allow man to go beyond that which seems to characterize him.

In this first volume we touch lightly upon tantrism as a precarious entity of man's evolution. We use the term precarious in the sense of temporary, since everything evolves, including tantrism. It couldn't be otherwise.

In the second volume we will touch upon the occult aspect of the human body, temporary receptacle of that which qualifies man as completely Divine. The body, qualified as a temple and as a cauldron of transformation of consciousness, as a bridge linking the human with the Divine, contains certain secrets conducive to the advancement of man towards his destiny. Some of these paths are ready to be revealed and tantrism will help us do so.

© Paume de Saint-Germain Publishing
Division of Orange Palm and Magnificent Magus Publications Inc.©
235 René Lévesque Boulevard East, Suite 310
Montréal, Québec, H2X 1N8, Canada
Telephone: (514) 255-8700
Facsimile: (514) 255-0478
E-mail: info@palmpublications.com
Web site: http://www.palmpublications.com